AF407756

Condensation of Thought

by

S.A Morris

Condensation of Thought

COPYRIGHT © 1997 by Stephen Arville Morris

All rights reserved. No part of this publication may be re-produced, distributed, or transmitted in any form or by any means, including photo-copying, recording, or other electronic or me-chanical methods, without the prior written permission of the publisher, except in the case of brief quotations embodied in critical reviews and certain oth-er noncommercial uses permitted by copyright law.

Printed In United States

In **Condensation of Thought**, *Stephen Arville Morris* distills the complexities of life into concise, thought-provoking reflections. This collection explores themes such as the power of words, the fleeting nature of life, and the quest for wisdom. Each unsorted, standalone thought invites deep contemplation and personal introspection. With elegant brevity, Morris emphasizes simplicity and clarity in communication, offering a compact yet rich tapestry of insights.

The man of few words sat silent while the man of few ideas talked on.

So what is this *Condensation of Thought?* What is the value of brevity? Saying the same thing and dwelling on the same idea in a multitude of ways is a futile attempt to exhaust a subject by insisting on the first and last word. It leaves no room to add or subtract. I believe it is far better to instigate thought than to end it and to stimulate a mind rather than fill it with conclusions.

It all begins with the power of words.

Words are nothing. Nothing tangible. Just the friction of wind through vocal chords, ink marks on paper or lines on a monitor. Yet words are everything. They move us to be proud, angry, happy, sad, excited and serene.

Words are the elements of thought. With them we transport ideas from one mind to another, from one time to another.

In the absence of discourse, all experience is fleeting. Undefined action is mere motion without meaning.

Yet a surplus of words can dilute substance and bury the very ideas we wish to display. Sometimes we say more by saying less. We clarify when we simplify.

A good thought can be stretched into a book or squeezed into a nugget. I prefer to squeeze.

Condensation of Thought is merely the process of wrapping ideas into an elegant and compact package of words to be passed on to you for your consideration.

Random thoughts …

The thoughts that follow are not sorted by topic or value or time of creation. In fact, they are intentionally unsorted. One idea does not lead to the next. Each is intended to be complete in itself. There is no pathway from beginning to end. The content is itself the destination.

Even though originality was always the goal, some of my thoughts may have unintentionally been borrowed from others and expressed in a new set of words. As Ralph Waldo Emerson so tactfully put it:

All of my best thoughts were stolen by the ancients.

A single drop...

is as much the substance of water as the combined oceans of the
world. And in a single life lies all the humanity of mankind. If one
person can be counted as a trifle, then an entire history of people
piled upon people won't add to a cat's whisker.

The successful rich business person outperforms his competition
with a combination of smart moves, discipline, hard work and lucky
breaks. Some are good people and some not so good. The rich, like
celebrity actors and athletes, should not be worshiped.

A business dynamo thrives in his environment, but then so does a weed.

Over the years we question where,
Where do we go once we die?
And over the years we answer there,
There's more to this than meets the eye.

The earth spins and circles the sun. The sun loops the Milky Way.
Plants and animals struggle to survive from day to day oblivious to
purpose. Man, of all the life forms on earth, has the feeling he is
going somewhere other than round and round.

To see others excel is to find possibilities in ourselves.

When we remember, we gather facts.
When we analyze, we find their meaning.
But when we create, we are most god-like.

The more possessions possessed, the more the possessor is possessed by his possessions.

You want to fit in. You want to be accepted. But you also want to stand out. If you know a better way, if you can write or sing a better tune, why hide it? Don't give in and go along just because it's easier. Sure, it's hard to swim upstream. Any dead body can float down. Don't live in someone else's world when you can create your own. You will never be able to change the world until you show the world it can't change you.

Religion is more a reflection of man than of religion's deity. If you want to truly know a person, you must understand what he believes. You then not only recognize who he is today, but who he will be tomorrow.

Never compromise the **core** of an issue. Concede only the frivolous. Half a loaf is still bread. But half a child is a corpse.

In our capitalistic society, you must allow some of us to make a lot of money to enable the rest of us to make enough. And those who do well must never be content while those who seek opportunity through work are denied.

Addiction is a disease. But it's not one you innocently catch. It's one you went out and got. That's why it's a stupid disease. It's self-inflicted.

Just because you believe what you say doesn't mean you are telling the truth. Isn't that the definition of delusional:

being so persuasive that you believe your own lies.

Wrong-Headed:

a person who brilliantly deduces a thousand conclusions from a false premise.

When you steal, you believe you acquire something for free, but you lose something in exchange. You give up part of your dignity as a human being. The spiritual loss, once discerned, far exceeds the material gain.

The fun part of having a dog, unlike your kids, is that you can spoil the heck out of him and not have to worry that someday he won't be able to go out and get a job. Remember, as you train your dog he is training you. He studies your routine and strategically lays down in a place where he can observe your comings and goings. He rewards your attention with a wagging tail or a facial lick. He doesn't care if no one likes you. He idolizes you because life is better that way. Oh, if only humans were a little more like dogs.

Money changes us. It empowers, it comforts, and it expands our opportunities. A rich man is not just a poor man with more money. He is a changed man. In fact, too much money can make a person eccentric. The poor, it seems, just haven't the means to afford such a luxury. They have to fit in and avoid being strange.

It used to embarrass me to say what I thought was the obvious truth until it occurred to me that with some people it wasn't so obvious. So much of what we believe is cloaked in a fabric of lies to present a story that the teller only wishes were true. History is full of disguises. A truth must be undressed to appreciate its naked beauty.

This crazy business provides me money while it steals my time, and as I get older, time becomes more valuable and evolves into the currency of preference.

The bird eats the lowly worm, but once the high flying bird dies, it's the worm that has the last meal.

Climate change is a fact and has been a fact for millions of years. Man's influence on climate is also a fact. So also are a host of other uncontrollable variables – the activities of the sun, the orbit of the earth, volcanic eruptions, and earthquakes. But political solutions should always be suspect. My theory is that global warming is greatly enhanced by all of that hot air coming out of Washington.

Can leadership disavow responsibility? If George Washington became lost while riding his horse, would he have blamed the horse?

Why do we value intelligence so highly? For some, the worst insult we could suffer is to be called stupid. Being called smart is a compliment. But an intelligent person without morals is just a more efficient monster.

Intelligence will accelerate your journey down any road, but wisdom will place you on the right road.

If I am homeless and come upon the house of another, what good does it do me to burn his house down?

A life of work instills a pride of achievement. We fill a place in our society. We fit in. We become known for what we do. My friend is an electrician, a lawyer, a doctor, or a business owner. When we grow old and quit work, we lose that identity.

As for me, in retirement, I don't have to be significant. I would settle for being relevant.

The one who scares me most in this world is not the murderer, the robber, the rapist or the vandal. These can all be stopped. The one I most fear is the well-meaning fool who leads us from light to dark, from the rational life to the irrational, and all in the name of a misunderstood higher good.So much of what this person does cannot be easily undone. We have seen them come and go, live and die, leaving us strapped with their cultural handcuffs. They are history's front page: *Karl Marx, Adolf Hitler, Mao Zedong, and a host of religious fanatics.*

They parade down Main Street as if it led to Heaven.

Some people make the world a better place by being in it, others by leaving it.

Peace is wonderful. Sustaining a war is perhaps the most horrible, devastating, and costly condition a people can ever suffer, with the possible exception of losing a war.

Find a profession that will satisfy your financial needs. Match your talents to the times you are born into. Today's professional athletes were yesterday's expendable soldiers. Our current celebrity actors and singers might have been modest farmers and merchants in centuries past. An ancient tribe would have had little use for the talents of today's academic. Misapplied skills go unappreciated. Keep your passion but employ your profession.

Every thinking person eventually comes to grips with his situation. If life were just so very long, the disbelievers would confess to not being self-made; the clergymen would doubt their obstinate faith. We all would snuggle comfortably around this warmth we call earth.

And as a cool wind howls at our backs, *we would smile and share our common life.*

You could spend your whole life apologizing for thoughtlessness, unkindness and so on. But that's like walking on your heels.

Go forward.

You bump your butt more often backing up.

Believing in God is a religion, but then so is not believing.

*I once tried atheism as a logical interpretation of a scientific world but soon had to give it up. I had myself convinced that the whole universe was a big accident. There was no plan, no origin, and no meaning to existence. But what I could not make myself believe was that **I** was a big fat accident. Any universe that had me in it was no accident. Realism had set in and my imaginary disbelief in spirituality became impossible to swallow. I had to leave atheism, the religion of chaos, to those who are not bothered by the fact of their own existence.*

BIG thoughts should be given in small doses.

A field cannot grow in a flood.

And poison can be made harmless if diluted.

We all seek satisfaction. But the satisfied man never produces anything beyond mediocrity.
Being uncomfortable in your situation is the first step to improving it.

No man will ever come between a woman and her child... nor should he. Women with men may be selfish but women with their children are selfless.

If you can't be kind, considerate, and generally good to the bone, take acting lessons.

I'm competitive for two reasons:
I like to win and **I hate to lose.**

The **only way** I found to be free from the desire of money is to have some. (The same goes for love, sex, and circus peanuts.)

There are two kinds of work: straight lines and circles. Linear work takes you from point A to point B. Something is accomplished. Circular activity can be just as strenuous yet nothing is achieved. The journey from point A back to point A is more a workout than work.

Since when did the person saying the thing matter more than the thing being said? All the endorsements of an issue clustered together have never formed the foundation of a truth.

Neither celebrity nor democracy can certify the veracity of an issue, only its popularity.

It's a nasty trick Nature plays upon women to first give them the extraordinary ability to feel life so much better than a man, and then send them through the agony of giving birth.

A mother's love is unconditional and absolute. As much as anything we encounter it is a wonder without reason. In moments of doubt we ask ourselves, "Why would anyone love *me* .... with all my imperfections?"

It is a wonder without reason.

What I like about the business world compared to sports is that, to be a winner, there doesn't have to be a loser. In fact, the best business deals are ones in which everyone wins, even if at different levels.

Anyone can be foolish, but it takes a really smart person to be an egregious fool.

Intelligence is to wisdom as talent is to success. The first you recognize; the second you appreciate.

Being a fast worker is not always productive. It could mean mistakes just happen faster.

If the world were dark
I'd be the sun
And shine for all to see.
And show what is
And what is not
For all eternity.

If the world were dry
I'd be the rain
And clean the filthy air.
And wash the bad
From precious good
So everything was fair.

But I'm not the sun
Nor the rain.
I'm just a simple man
Who shines a light
And tidies up
And does what one man can.

The focus as to the value of our work should be on the *work* itself,
not on us.

Why not do as our creator did and produce a masterpiece, leaving
everyone to wonder who did this?

The question is not: "What is the meaning of life?" The question is:
"I'm alive. Now what am I going to do about it?" Don't ponder the
unknowable. Seek the attainable.

Everywhere you go, the center of the universe goes with you.
Objectivity is in the mind's eye.

Doing what you love and getting it to pay is better than only doing
what you love or only getting paid.

No one is immune to death and you don't have to be in a war zone to die.

Your personal security is only as strong as the goodwill of the person standing next to you.

None of us are as good as we should be or as bad as we could be. But all of us are as kind and as generous and as hateful and as selfish as we intend to be. The world doesn't make us who we are. We do.

Listening to a sweet song or reading a fine poem can stimulate the senses. Where do these creators find these intense feelings?

Everyone wants to write like a poet,

but no one wants to suffer.

Worry is not completely worthless.

It is the prediction of calamity that serves to prevent it.

A government that has the power to protect us from all our enemies both foreign and domestic has the power to become our enemy. A government that confiscates our wealth and then hands it back to us treats us as children, or even worse, as cattle. We can only be free if our government is constrained. Tie the government's hands or it will surely tie yours.

You can populate the world with millions of people, but still feel all alone without a god.

I am only partly of this human world, like *melody to music* composed before my birth, or *an idea from a thought* that was not my thought.

Write about the past with accuracy.

Write about the future with creativity.

Only a liar writes creatively about the past

And postulates the future with accuracy.

As an entrepreneur, I expect to compete in the marketplace against anyone, but not with the government, against everyone.

Those who do not appreciate their freedom will surely lose it. The one who will slip it away from us is always the one who distracts us with security, satisfaction, and guaranteed services.

When I was younger, I used to say I was *cursed* with a poor memory. Now I sometimes think I was *blessed* with a poor memory.

If I recalled too clearly and too often all the insults, cold shoulders, and outright evil deeds that have been thrown my way, I surely would be bitterly sad. It's easy for me to forget these wrongs and begin fresh each new day without dragging around old baggage of worn-out clothes from another time and place. Happiness, then, is as much a form of amnesia as it is fond memories.

How do we ever see eye-to-eye in this society when we have the far left who view government as almighty God dispensing justice and provisions to the common man while the far right view government as their low I.Q. cousin who may be sitting on inherited wealth but could never function in a competitive world? Perhaps the human race should agree to split up into two species to see which one survives. My money is on the socialists. After they run out of their own stuff, they will conquer the other species to get their stuff.

The socialist hates capitalism because it is based on human selfishness rather than altruism. The capitalist hates socialism because it is based on delusion rather than reality.

If movie-making equipment had been invented 5,000 years ago, the Jews would never have written the Bible. They would have filmed it.

Life is the summation of what you make it to be and what it makes you to be. Don't ever forget that in your hands is half the formula.

Ideas are like human beings: it's easier to shoot one down than to create one.

I have a habit of getting up out of bed at two o'clock in the morning for about an hour to read. My mind is actually more focused in the middle of the night with few diversions. It calms any anxiety stirring in my brain, clears my mind, and allows me to go back to bed and sleep like a rock. My wife thinks I should talk to my doctor of this and ask his help. On my last scheduled visit I did mention it to the doctor, who happens to be a long time neighbor and friend. He offered to write a prescription for a medication that would keep me asleep throughout the entire night. But I told him I actually liked my one-hour reading session that cleared my head and introduced many fine thoughts. He said, " I'm aware of your clear head and fine thoughts. Take the medication! " He really never said that. His facial expression did.

Ever since George Hudson suggested the idea back in 1895, people have questioned the benefit of daylight saving time. They say it's like cutting off a blanket at one end and sewing it on to the other. You are not going to be any warmer. But I believe it teaches us that time is relative and not absolute. Time is not based on the authority of the sun and the earth and the solar system, but rather on the authority of the state. It teaches us that the time is whatever the government says it is.

To be happy, you need only find what you like to do and do more of it. **To build character**, you must determine what you feel needs to be done, and dutifully do it, regardless of consequences.

As a business owner over the years, I have employed thousands of American citizens and paid a great quantity of dollars in taxes. And not once in all those years has anyone from the government stopped by to say, "thank you." It's like no one appreciates the usefulness of their car until the engine dies.

We gain material wealth by acquisition. Love and happiness, on the other hand, are not attained by acquiring, but by sharing.

Conceited Intellect...

I've found that those who think they are smart are the easiest to deceive, if you are inclined to deceive them.

If you have a small cake, no matter how you slice it, you still don't have much to eat.

Biographies are so important because every good life tells a story and every bad life an even better one.

In the restaurant business, as an outsider looking in, I believe the best way to be successful is to have slightly higher prices with food to die for than low prices with food that makes you die.

I'm convinced that everyone has his element, if he can only find it before he dies. Some are great leaders and some are great builders and inventors. Some great athletes. But the greatness does not transfer to all the other elements. When we are in our element, we fulfill our purpose in nature, and that glow of fulfillment is all the reward we need.

It's funny how "funny" can change. When I was four or five years old, I used to think that ringing someone's doorbell and running away was the funniest thing in the world. It was hilarious. Just thinking about it would make me giggle. Now that I'm older and mature, I find no humor in it at all. It's not funny. It's annoying. And as of a few years ago I quit doing it.

A *working dog* believes his job is to guard and protect his owner. A *pet dog* is convinced that the owner is there to protect *him*.

To be an absolute ruler, you don't have to be a genius or physically strong, or have any special talent. To be a Hitler or a Stalin or a Saddam Hussein, you must adhere to a simple callous philosophy I'll call the "Mafia Morality": reward your friends and destroy your enemies. The dead offer no resistance. The living obey if they fear you. And the only requisite sacrifice is the essential one: your humanity. Although you will continue to speak and act as a human, you continue to reflect light and appear as human, you metamorphose into an anti-human, a monster. You become the hated enemy of the human race. Every free and noble spirit under your spell will unfortunately fold up like flower pedals shrouded by frigid darkness.

The good man and the bad man are the same man.
Look too closely at the cheat and we find qualities of a saint.
Look too closely at the saint and we find elements of a cheat.

The brave intellect is an audible voice of reason in a room of whispers.

Pleasure is a scratch for an itch, not the absence of the itch.

When someone gives you a binary choice of A or B, remember C and D, neither and both. Don't let the question frame the answer.

Time is like a big eraser on a chalkboard. Just when you feel that things are terribly bad or things are fantastically good or that your life will go on forever, **here comes that eraser.**

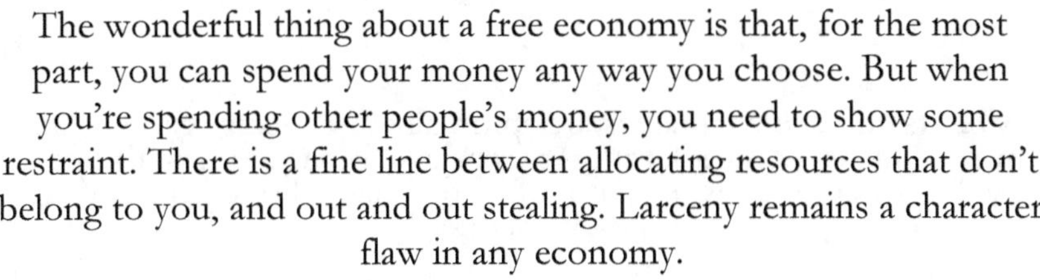

The wonderful thing about a free economy is that, for the most part, you can spend your money any way you choose. But when you're spending other people's money, you need to show some restraint. There is a fine line between allocating resources that don't belong to you, and out and out stealing. Larceny remains a character flaw in any economy.

In retrospect, I regret less the doing than the undone, less the trying than the untried.

The world is more beautiful and elegant than I can possibly know. How many thousands of wonders have fallen from my glance while staring at the few I have seen?

Atheists and even agnostics are spiritually lost. Being with others, many others, is only a temporary reprieve. Being alone with one's self is always the test of faith. Only the man who has his god is never alone.

Might does not make right but it does make winners.

In time of war, don't concern yourself with right and wrong. The winners will sort all that out after they bulldoze the dead.

All wisdom is foolish to a fool's ear. When you educate a foolish mind, you end up with an educated fool.

The one good thing about having to deal with fools is that it gives you a better appreciation of your own intellect.

A hundred years hence the truth will become apparent: American franchises and other business entities of free trade have done more for world peace than foreign aid and the State Department put together. Capitalism, based on greed and selfishness, has harnessed human individualism and self determination to create a better world for everyone.

We owe so much to those who came before. Our parents are paid through the gifts we give to our children. It is **love** that stokes the fire and keeps the flame aglow. It lights our way and warms us from within.

Whenever I read about people being persecuted because they are the wrong race or religion, or because they sold sex for money or ingested a funny substance, I have to remind myself: We are all just a bunch of monkeys down from the tree – and we haven't been down for that long. What silly creatures we are for believing we are so godlike.

Is it foolish to have faith? Or is it even possible not to have faith?

I have faith that I will wake in the same bed and to the same world tomorrow that I go to sleep in today. I have faith that the sun will rise, the laws of physics remain in place, and my mind and body are a continuation of the night before.

The point is, I have faith because I have no proof.

Beware of those people who are so certain about the uncertainties of life. They may lie to **you** just as they have to themselves.

Truth and its revelation...

We all have our secrets. We all have our privacy. Some thoughts never breach the skin of the mind into the public forum. That's OK. Thankfully, mere thoughts are not subject to prosecution.

I don't need to learn my neighbor's sexual fantasies, or his prejudices, or what he despises, or what terrifies him. I don't expect him to reveal everything about himself, nor should he expect any more of me. Concealing the truth is not the same as not confronting it. If, for example, nature is not deterministic, if it is probabilistic instead, then accepting the best possible explanation means changing our minds and making personal adjustments. Nothing is worse than blind faith in something untrue.

I don't respect people who fear the truth. And when I fear knowledge of what is true, I don't respect myself. We can only create a better world once we clearly envision the present one.

There is no such thing as a bad mattress if the sex is good.

People who claim they never get any lucky breaks probably wouldn't recognize opportunity if they sat on it and it bit them on the butt.

Death is nothing to the dead. They neither see it, fear it, nor ponder it. The dead don't smile or sing or watch the morning sky. They don't complain or feel pain. They neither regret the past nor worry for the future. They care not in the least of our affairs. The dead are gone from this life forever. They are like a day now past. Death is a loss to the living. A lesson that all is temporary.

Of all the animals, only man has a sense of history. The others merely carry habit from one moment to the next. Our long memory stretches back thousands of years to the earliest written words and cave-wall drawings. But memory is not history without objective perspective. History is valuable when it blesses what was right and condemns what was wrong, and when it teaches values that can be used in the present from a frame of reference in the past.

Was it God who created man or was it man who created God? We can take a stand either way but that doesn't change a thing. Subjective reality is what we believe it to be. Objective reality doesn't care what we believe.

In a complex world, you don't achieve the good by **eliminating** the bad, but by having the good **dominate** the bad.

The opposite of smart is stupid, while the opposite of wise is foolish. I would rather be wise than smart and I would rather go through life stupid than foolish. Stupid is a fault of nature whereas foolish would be of my own making. Even a stupid person can be wise if he knows he is stupid.

There aren't dishonest people in the absolute sense. But there are people who do dishonest things from time to time. The distinction is noteworthy. We can be neither devils nor angels any more than we can be dogs or cats. We can be only human. Acting like something is not being that something. Your actions describe you, not define you.

Some people act and some people protest and call it action.

If your employees don't like you, that's life. But if your kids don't like you, that's a lost life.

Honor gives in to greed not because greed is superior but because character is weak.

If you love yourself you will always be loved.
If you love another you will be worthy of love.

What type of character do you want to have? That's easy.

Become the sort of person you wish was your best friend.

Certain subjects are meant to be light and silly. If you ponder a joke too deeply, you can literally suck the humor out of it.

You don't cure a drug problem with legislation any more than you cure cancer by making it illegal.

Some say, *Don't worry. Be happy.* Worry frays the nerves and sucks the energy out of you. It can turn your mood blue and your hair white. So what good does it do to worry? I understand a lot of things we spend time worrying about never happen. But isn't that the point?

I exhale the remaining vapors of a weary day as evening rushes in to
fill the void of light.

The mind becomes mindless and insulates the senses from the
sweet smell of life.

It's easy not to see.
It's easy not to feel.
It's easy not to think.

Habit eats away the meat of life and leaves a bony summary to
structure what was lost.

Routine removes uncertainty but sanitizes adventure's dusty face.

Putting a cigarette to your lips is like sipping slow poison. Each
morning you awake more frail than the day before. It is a dirty nasty
smelly senseless and deadly habit. Yes, but doesn't it feel so cool to
interrupt a thought, inhale deeply, take a long puff, and continue
the thought? Isn't it better to pause and reflect rather than to stream
through a conversation? OK, so sip a cup of coffee or tea, smell
your fingers or stare at your feet. Mannerisms don't have to kill you.

If your goal is equality, go to the cemetery.
Everyone there is equal and no one complains.

Hold your head high, not for appearances, but so that you can better see where you are going.

The fallacy of excess....

Be very cautious of those who say, *if a little is good, more is better.* In the case of alcohol it can lead to alcoholism. With chocolate, it can cause a bloated upset stomach. When people argue that if some immigration has been good, allowing millions to enter the country is even better. Never mind the effect on schools, social programs, employment, transportation and culture. Ask the Chinese about living in a crowded country of over a billion people and how it affects human value and freedom.

When a doctor writes a prescription, he determines the quantity based on individual patient characteristics such as age and weight. The doctor knows that too much of a good medication can be deadly.

If someone is right about most issues, should you trust he will be right on all issues? Of course not.

In math they call it *extrapolating the curve* or estimating from values within a known range by assuming that the estimated value follows logically from the known values.

Let's not forget the fallacy that *going twice as fast will get you there in half the time.* In some instances like on a winding road you might not get there at all.

Never assume that more of a good thing is a better thing. It is only better until it is too much. You only reach *excess* after blindly passing *enough* along the way.

Belief should have no more authority than the hypothesis of the scientist. It should be used as a key to open doors, not to lock them.

Exaggeration:

Too strong, thus wrong.

When struggling to do what is difficult, try to do it in slow motion.

Being quick is either a sign of mastery, or a method to conceal awkwardness.

The stock market usually doesn't shoot
up as quickly as it can collapse down,

which only proves that panic is more powerful than euphoria.

Today I feel like a turtle who tried to win a race, but ultimately became the **soup**.

Woe to the man whose only place of worship is between a woman's legs. Without sense, the senses lead to ruin. Pleasure is not a destination, but the fuel to motivate. It's a propellant when tethered by moderation, but an explosive when randomly ignited.

An insect such as an ant or a bee will pursue how best to serve the ant hill or hive, but it has no freedom to question why.

You can ask yourself "how questions" all day long and brilliantly fill your head with knowledge. But until you question why, you will never attain wisdom and truly exercise free will.

If Aesop had written for the sake of popularity long epics instead of brief fables, the world would have traded a master story teller for a second rate windbag.

When you apply black and white solutions to problems tinted with gray, you end up with more gray problems. Examples are laws limiting the drinking age to 21 and the illegal drug fiasco. Good intentions don't justify bad policy. Doing the wrong thing is never better than doing nothing. The law of unintended consequences always catches up to simple-minded fixes. College kids binge on booze in defiance of a hypocritical law. The illegal drug business flourishes due to artificial circumstances. Never send in a bigger skunk to cover up a bad smell.

Approach the unknown with the tentacles of an octopus, enveloping it from every side, and seeing it with as many eyes as your own imagination can project.

In a single poker hand, combining a lot of luck with a little skill generally prevails over a little luck and a lot of skill. But during an extended time, the skillful player loses little when he loses and wins big when he wins. So it's not always how *many times* you win or lose, but how *much* each time. With seven players, you can expect to lose six times for each win. Those who persist in playing every hand to the finish, will probably finish last.

Condensation of Thought

Surely a nation suffers when its fools are prosperous.

The one who labors from 8 to 5 is a worker. The one who stays at home and sends his money to work is a capitalist. The one who goes to work from 8 to 5 but really only works from 9 to 11 is a socialist, paid by the government.

Always overlook petty offenses.
But always look them over.

If I don't agree with your argument, saying it louder doesn't help.

People who worship power have no moral qualities because they are fully aware that they can lie, cheat, steal, and murder their way to power and, if power is attained, no one will hold them accountable. Power trumps purity. Hitler knew all his sins would be forgiven and all his mistakes forgotten if he could win the war. With total power, he could write his own history book and only the losers would look bad.

Sometimes it seems our day-to-day problems are not solved as much by great thought as by cold cash.

Everyone complains about their government: the good ones for being taxed and the bad ones for being punished.

When I was young I raised hell. When I got older I raised children. The pendulum of pain swings both directions.

It is better to admit your mistakes than to suffer others who are happy to point them out.

It's odd that so many confuse sexuality with morality. Sex in itself is neither good nor evil, but in its application can be either. Morality can only exist when there is an intelligent mind considering options. It must have the freedom to choose without regard to reward or punishment. While sexuality can bring pleasure, morality begets nobility and dignity.

The first economic rule of government in a free market system is to keep the market free. It must be kept free from needless burdensome rules, government favoritism, unfair taxation, monopolies, and strategies that would impede competition. But no governmental interference in economic affairs or *laissez-faire* is a formula that would destroy freedom rather than promote it.

The government must also keep the labor market free. Labor should be free to sell its services to the highest bidder but not to control the market through compulsory unionization.

When companies or labor unions are allowed to monopolize, the market loses its flexibility, its ability to adjust to change.

The genius of capitalism is its ability to evolve through trial and error with competition to make life better for everyone. It does not make everyone equal, but then neither does nature.

Our creator kissed our cheek, and sent us to play in the world. *And when you are tired,* He says, *and no longer can pull apples from the tree, or build castles with mud from the shoulders of the stream, come back to me and tell me of your wonderful day in the backyard sun.*

There is a mathematics underpinning the entire universe. It's remarkable. From relationships of matter and energy to probability theory of positions, the physical world is formulated. God, if he exists, is not a carpenter. He's a mathematician.

Those who think on their seat
And not on their feet,
Must follow and heed
Those who can lead.

Never let anyone browbeat you. If you don't understand it and they can't adequately explain it, then they don't understand it.

Do not make a man more in death than he was in life. You don't honor a memory by creating an illusion.

Never fear adversity. That's when we do our best work.

The greatness of the Bible or the Koran comes not from being the word of God, but from being the inspired work of man. In reading these books, remove the culture and retain the wisdom.

Poetry is low fat prose. Stripped of excess, it must be precise and clear – pleasing in sound – fulfilling in substance. It must bite into our nerves and shake us from routine. Poetry must never just be pretty melody with rhyming gibberish. Sometimes a poem is hard to define simply because it was forced to rhyme.

You call a conference to either make a decision you cannot find on your own, or to sell a decision you have found on your own.

Political persuasion...

I am both liberal and a conservative: liberal when we are spending someone else's money, conservative when it's my own.

Some physicists confuse mathematical possibility with physical reality. If you chomp down on the wrong theory, you end up with a belly full of air.

If scientists find evidence of life on millions of planets in the universe, will that dismiss the question of God or only enhance it?

The realist dismisses our life experience in a most direct way:

Get born…

Cry…

Eat… Poop…

Eat… Poop…

Eat… Poop…

Eat… Poop…

Eat… Poop…

Die.

Truth has *a* life of its own, independent of the mind conceiving it.

Believing the world is flat doesn't make the earth any less round.

When dogs get together and have puppies, are they married? It is like marriage. When birds form a union and build a nest, are they married? Sort of, but not exactly. When two men or two women live together, have sex, open a joint account, can they be married? How about a three-some: two men/one woman or two women/one man? Sort of, but not exactly. You can give gay people all the rights of married couples. You can give them more rights. Just don't call it a marriage. Being **like** something else is not **being** something else.

Never come between a person and his beloved self-interest.
You may get run over and it won't even be *personal*.

Everything we know of the past is tainted with interpretation.
The one who records history has the power to change history.

In the long history of the human race of renowned people with great ideas, discoveries, and accomplishments, we only care about what the people did, what they were good at doing, not what they could *not* do. Perhaps Napoleon could not play the piano and Washington could not sing. All of us have a million things we do not do well. What interests us are the things people do very well. Don't try to excel in a card game with a poor hand. Focus on what you do better than anyone, even if no one asks for it. Work to develop the talent unique to yourself.

Sara's   birthday...
On this, your special day, the earth has rounded the sun once again.

And as a grand clock that chimes,
We chime to celebrate your birthday.
Light the candles. Sing a song.
Serve the cake. Pound the drum.
Stir the air and wake the world.
The flowers and trees and all the ornaments of nature glow in the

Joyous sunshine of this, your special day.

A good salesperson will be just as interested in what you need to buy as he is in what he wants to sell. He connects the want with the wanted.

Do not put justice above all things. For the obsessively just person will have few friends, only acquaintances. The cold impartial referee is never loved, only respected. Instead, use love in all things, especially in the love of justice, freedom, and wisdom. The radiance of love illuminates experience to give it value. Love changes all because it changes us.

Keep your "crapola" detector going at all times. It's a mechanism we all have that separates the "crap" from the "ola", the chaff from the wheat, the bad stuff from the good.

On JFK....

He was a politician because he had to be, but he was a poet because he could be. He used language to make freedom fashionable again.

Inside every communist who believed in the morality of Marxism, huddled a spirit yearning to be free.

There was a sweet little old lady in the senior living center where my mother lived who was one of the few single women still driving a car. She was always helpful in transporting her friends but was insistent on one rule: she would not make a left turn. On-coming traffic made it too stressful to risk such a maneuver.

So even though two wrongs don't make a right, surprisingly, three rights do make a left and the sly old lady had found a way to drive almost anywhere without the anxiety of a left turn.

Sleeping **1/3** of the day is not a waste.

Not being completely awake for the other **2/3**'s is.

Always hire people who are smarter than you. That way, when they do smart things, they make you look smart.

I don't need someone else around to make me look stupid.

Before the age of photography, paintings were all we had to depict our world. Now we can freeze-frame every second.

Today photography is best when picturing things as they are. Paintings should depict possibilities.

Why is human life of value? Because that which dispenses value on others must itself be of value. The opposite is a *reductio ad absurdum*.

When you speak, be careful when making fun of yourself. Your enemies will view this as a confession.

This be a worldly lesson
no nation should neglect:
weakness attracts aggression
while strength commands respect.

Fashions, technologies, and entire cultures are continuously changing. Trends are like road maps, until they untrend. They then appear more like nostalgic chapters in a history book. Unfortunately, by the time some people catch the wave of the future, the future is waving goodbye.

Sincere praise from an enemy is the ultimate expression of respect.

We are tiny specs in a giant universe.
If the earth were a dog, we'd all be fleas.

I cry because I haven't a thousand lives to live, yet I waste the one I have.

On unjust laws....

Never let a rulebook prevent you from doing what is right.

With the inexperienced, you answer his questions.

With the experienced, you question his answers.

The best way to discredit bad ideas is with better ones.

Values, to be worthwhile, must be long term, though our lives are not.

Make yourself useful and you will go places. Make yourself *indispensable*, and you won't be able to go.

Singularly crafted carbon cells
Differentiate one from many.
While patterned code
And social load
Meld everyone to any.

The wise use the intellect of others to supplement their own. They read.

Give a person some ownership in the land, and not only will he work for it, he will fight for it. When we own property, it also owns us, and we do not part easily.

If what you do is not fun, you need to seek out ways to make it fun.
If you can't make it fun, **don't do it.**

The fastest way to have a *former wife* is to introduce her as your
current wife.

Extremists who preach hatred, violence, and intolerance don't
worship God.

They pray to the Devil and call him God.

How do you define "rich"? Whatever amount of money you have,
you always want more. Is it when you live in a house with no
mortgage? Are you rich when you can quit working and not starve?
It may have something to do with your desire for the things money
can buy. A bigger appetite calls for a bigger wallet. A person is rich
by my definition when he can afford to tell the rest of the world to
go to hell. I'm not saying you should ever do that, but it is a
comfort to know that you could. Money may not buy love and
happiness, but it can purchase a lot of independence and freedom. I
suppose I would define "rich" more as a state of mind rather than a
measure of money. You are rich when your wants don't surpass
your means, when you covet no one's property, and when you fully
appreciate the beautiful gifts you already possess.

John F. Kennedy did two things that shallow people never understood:

1. *To build the economy and increase overall tax revenue to the treasury, he called for lower tax rates.*

2. *In order to preserve the peace, he prepared the country for war.*

Amazingly, there are still both Democrats and Republicans who can't understand these apparent contradictions.

Other bits of irony:

To be happy, strive to make others happy.
To view your situation more clearly, close your eyes.
To succeed more often, you have to be willing to fail more often.
The early bird gets the worm, but the early worm gets eaten.

Beware of statistics. You have to see beyond the numbers. Attempting to measure quality with quantity is like trying to appreciate a beautiful woman by calculating her height, weight, and circumference.

Achievement...
It's the little successes, not the big ones, that make life worth living.
There are more of them and the satisfaction in the long run is about
the same.

I lost a friend the other day.
He simply vanished, passed away.
His body buried, goodbyes said,
Now part of me is also dead.

Books are a form of barf....

Jotting things down is therapeutic. To purge your brain of a
smorgasbord of ideas, you have to regurgitate them onto a sheet of
paper. Thus writing is quite simply a process of throwing up
bottled-up thoughts. Do authors write for their readers or for
themselves?

Style and substance is the difference between knowing **how** to write
and knowing **what** to write.

On spirituality...

The fact that each of us has perspective, that you are you and no one else, is an intuitive argument, not for all of us objectively, but for each of us subjectively, for a commanding intelligence in the universe, call it what you will.

If I were a mere robot of nature, I would not be me (nor you you).

Life is a personal experience, not an objective one. We are appointed actors to play the part of a person who owns our circumstance.

To sense our creator's existence is to confirm our own.

Can we truly be real if there is no before or after? It is our subjective world that implies the reality of the objective one. Our only evidence is a spiritual footprint.

Life has many secrets, but for me, the greatest mystery in the world is that I am in it.

Everyone wonders where they go when they die.
No one cares where they were before conception.

If you consider losing as a way of learning, then each loss is a step up instead of down. Losing is a process. Winning is a place.

Failures are temporary.

Victories are forever.

Relax. Enjoy the day. Feel the love and sense the humor. It's always there to be found.

But don't get too comfortable.

You won't be here for long.

Law schools can have a corrupting influence on a young person's mind. They can sometimes alter their intellectual honesty. The truth no longer matters, only its perception. That's what makes winners and losers. It becomes acceptable to stretch and twist the truth or avoid it altogether. If a jury perceives the truth as the lawyer presents it then why bother with the unadulterated version. Only the superior intellect can overcome this perverse training and not interpret everything in this superficial way.

Some go to law school because they understand good laws make good societies, others because they are looking for loopholes. These rascals often go into politics.

No boss in his right mind is going to pay you a lot more than you are worth. That's why you become an entrepreneur. You have to eliminate the boss.

Being an entrepreneur involves passing through two very different phases. The first is being known as the **most reckless fool** in town. The second, if you ever get there, is being praised as a **visionary intellect.** Only the second makes the first worth enduring.

On organized religion...

Be cautious in visiting any place where you are asked to check your intellect at the front door and suspend all judgment during your stay. Religion should be a quest, not a place.... a discussion, not a resolution.

Diversity…

Don't fret about your peculiarities: your height, your skin, the size of your nose, your sexual nature. The things that make you different make you unique and make you special. And differences don't make you better than anyone else unless you use your differences to make a difference.

The shorter the vision, the shorter the reach.
The longer the vision, the longer the reach.

Our continuing performance is not a matter of building one perfection and then going to another, but rather the making of choices, none of which are perfect.

In polite society where you are careful to consider the feelings of others, too much honesty can make the natives very uncomfortable. Do not strive to always tell the truth, only to know it. A little fiction can prevent a lot of friction.

A view from 1997 …

The marketplace will dictate what you will be doing five years from now – not Bill Clinton – not Bill Gates. Why? Because markets represent aggregate wisdom. Even those individuals who are smarter than anyone else are not smarter than everyone else.

The only time there's no way out is when there's no way in. If you got yourself in, you can get yourself out.

Intelligence is like an infinite hall of mirrors into which we drag a thought twisting and turning to expose all of its angles and sides. Some can go farther down this corridor than others. And some are content to view only one surface of an idea and believe what they see is all there is. Intelligence then is more than procedural or recollective or analytical or reflective. It is a merger of knowledge and possibility, and at its best creative.

When I was young, the thrill of danger was too seductive to be checked by the fear of death.

But the older I get, the more I am persuaded that I might die after all.

If we no longer try to dream, it is from fear of disappointment.

Idealism can be a flight of fantasy or shuttle to the future. When we compare what is to what should be, some see a disjointed world and collapse into the emptiness of lonely despair. Others discern the chance to build a new reality, and are galvanized by the spirit of purpose.

A leader must have vision and influence. The better the vision and the greater his influence of others, the better the leader. A leader is not an operations manager. His job is not to help people to move. His job is to turn them so they move in the right direction.

When I die, please bury my faults with me even if you have to dig a much bigger hole.

The man who doesn't pray to something is lost. But he who is sure to whom he prays is also lost (but possibly happier).

Men of power concern themselves with how history

will judge them. But in the final analysis, they are merely judged as dead.

Have you ever dangled a slice of bacon in front of your dog just to watch him salivate?

Nothing is more frustrating than to have a vision and not be in position to act on it.

Tomorrow is too late for today.
Our time will have passed away.
And all that has been, never again,
Our time will have passed away.

Take the time before the time takes thee.

One dose of experience is worth a dozen lectures.

It is easier to read someone else's ideas and question them, rather than think your own and live the consequences.

It is difficult to be blindly religious and at the same time be a good scientist, if science can be defined as a search for materialistic truth. The devoutly religious have already come to an early pragmatic conclusion of the ultimate questions presumably because life is short and an active life begs for resolution. When stumped, they always plug God in as the answer. The inquisitive investigator won't be successful doing that. So the well-adjusted scientist does not live **in** doubt as much as he must live **with** doubt. He coexists with uncertainty but without frustration.

History, art, politics, and philosophy are not the concerns of the famished and homeless. The appetite of the mind will always be subservient to that of the stomach. You can't pursue "wants" until you satisfy "needs".

I don't remember being born.
I won't remember being dead.
The in-between is clearly seen
As merely thoughts within my head.

As hand puppets on a stage
We share laughter, joy, rage.
But when the hand is pulled away
And we no longer have a say
The universe reclaims its dust
But not the hand of consciousness.
From where and to where does the spirit go?
I don't know. I don't know. I don't know.

In business, there's always a money trail. Follow that and you'll find out who's doing the business and who's getting the business.

It's rarely the stupid people who get us into the most trouble. They lack the means and imagination to cause

great havoc. The major problems come from those who are smart but lack wisdom. And what is wisdom but

the art to see beyond the moment and through the eyes of others.

The ultimate fate of life is death. Though one life may go sooner, the rest will follow thereafter. Our creator made us all mortal, not to belittle the experience, but to resolve it. Every life is a story, a beginning and an end. There seems to be no permanence in the physical universe except for the laws that govern it. And one imperative is that time changes everything, except the past, where one life is touched and forever altered by even the temporary existence of another.

Those possessed with a genuine desire to help others will *lead*. Those eager to exploit others for self-benefit will invariably *mislead*.

To the cell phone user, the whole world is a phone booth, to the dismay of everyone else.

Running a business …

Your business policy should be: Make it easy, fun, interesting and rewarding for your customers to do business with you. There will be bad customers just as there are bad employees or even bad businesses. Don't ever let your worst customers or employees dictate the policy for all the rest.

Sincerity doesn't make you right just as faith doesn't make something true.

My instincts tell me that hating someone is stupid, self-destructive, and a waste of time. But oh boy does it feel good for a while.

The definition of death is *having no future*, and the living dead are the most pathetic.

Only fools argue over a statement of fact (when it can be resolved by research).

Without death we lack the impetus for resolution.

Does God exist? I **do** care but I **don't** know.

My dog doesn't even care. She probably believes I'm her god. But it seems we are only aware of God, a creator, an all-knowing intelligence, when we are at our highest level of consciousness. Perhaps that should tell us something.

If there is a God, he is watching us always. But if there is no God, then it is up to us to nobly safeguard the human race and the earth we dwell upon. If not us, then who?

We all struggle to satisfy our daily needs, to fix immediate problems, to make our lives ever more comfortable. These short-term fixes lead to short-term thinking. Only someone who believes in God and an afterlife will take a long-term view of history despite his terminal life span.

I stand before the future, intimidated but exhilarated, as an unknowing child, stepping into a world made large through imagination.

Although one person can always make a difference, life is a collaborative affair. Americans need Russians, the French need the English, and yes, the Jews need the Muslims and vice versa. As in evolution, diversity and variety help to ensure survival by acclimating to change. Environments and situations forever change. We need each other to do what we need to do and to do it well.

There are three things you need to know about this idea:

1.   Always number your ideas.
2.   Always present them in a sequence.
3.   Never present more than three at a time.

Note: Use footnotes to explain yourself.

Cognitive Dissonance…

It is far better to be right than to be consistent. Sometimes you have to break a bad promise or tell a virtuous lie in the pursuit of a greater good. The hard part is knowing when. Deductive reasoning is insufficient when you must concurrently balance two contradictory principles with only a single brain. In short, it is like two dogs fighting inside one house for dominance.

Admonition to employees:

Treat all expenses like it's <u>your</u> money. Treat all income like it isn't.

Wouldn't it be odd if we had already completed a previous life and now find ourselves residing in a neurotic hell? Fear is the monster we must subdue, or it surely will devour the whole of us, one bite at a time.

America's current president always seems to be America's response to its last president. Let's start for example with Eisenhower. A renowned and successful military man replaced a politician, Truman, who was fighting the Korean war, had fired General McArthur for insubordination, and was combating creeping communism both within the USA and around the world. The elder Eisenhower was replaced with Kennedy, a young vigorous and charismatic leader promising to get America moving again after a perceived *laissez-faire* president who spent too much time playing golf. The Kennedy/Johnson team was replaced by Nixon, who was a *law and order* proponent during a time of civil rights and Viet Nam war protests. The disgraced Nixon/Ford presidency was replaced by Carter, a respected born-again Christian who promised never to lie to the American people. A perceived weak and confused Carter was followed by Reagan, representing strength and enlightened economic reform. Reagan and Bush, the old guys, were followed by Clinton, a much younger and charismatic progressive who focused on domestic inequality. Clinton, the impeached president, was replaced with G. W. Bush, another born-again Christian not burdened with an immoral sexual past. Bush *the war president* was followed by Obama *the peace loving socialist*. Obama *the apologist* and *leader-from- behind* in foreign affairs and a domestic economic catastrophe was followed by billionaire businessman Trump, who promised to drain the swamp and straighten out the economic mess left by his socialist predecessor.

And so the story goes.

The entire future of the human race begins with a simple erection and a social connection.

There are more lies told with numbers than were ever with mere words. Numbers have credibility. Quantity can be measured. Words are vague, changeable, and less trusted. Dress a lie in numbers and few will see it. Clothe a truth in words and see how the fools chatter and chatter and tear it to shreds.

A conversation requires a commitment to listen.

Two monologs do not make a dialog.

If you want people to like you, if you want people to want to be around you, don't focus on making yourself look good. Make the other guy feel good about himself.

An English bulldog is basically a large stomach walking around on four little legs. But he has a lot of character and he has even more charisma.

My bulldog imposed a triangular love affair within my family. I loved my wife. My wife loved the bulldog. And the bulldog was crazy about me. The occasional backflow kept it all in balance.

Society defines us more than we wish to admit.

The king of the crowd on Pauper Street is mere minion to the elite on High Street.

We compromise, we rationalize, forgive misdeeds, excuse misconduct. When do we stand firm? When our heels are at the precipice?

The leaning brings a great mass down.

Pleasure is a sensation. Happiness is a sensation wrapped in a thought. Pleasure can be as simple as eating an ice cream sundae. Happiness is believing that it won't be the last one you ever eat.

The business world is one of results. People are not interested in what you say unless they admire what you do.

You cannot make a poor man rich by making a rich man poor unless you resort to armed robbery. And even that process fades when you run out of unarmed rich men.

Justice …

Equality of outcome is not the definition of justice. It is the definition of mediocracy. **Diversity of outcome** means that some will do better than others. Forcing mediocracy by artificially promoting less qualified candidates over more qualified ones is a formula for failure. There is an old saying, *It doesn't matter if a cat is black or white, so long as it catches mice.* Hiring the most qualified regardless of race, religion, or gender gives us the best results. A just society or economy is a meritorious one: select the best and bring out the best in the best. Competition creates losers but losers are not insignificant. They are enablers helping to create the success of others. Progress depends just as much on losers as it does on winners. In that system we will find our definition of justice.

The English language has transformed from individual words to word clusters and acronyms. *Morning has broken* replaces *sunrise*. *Have a good day* substitutes for *goodbye*. The computer industry has created more acronyms than computers: html, pdf, pc, www, and so on. Our founding fathers from just over 200 years ago would need a translator to communicate with us today. If only good ideas could multiply as fast as new expressions, which too often substitute for good ideas.

Tolerance of small differences is not a retreat from one's principles but an affirmation of one's character. If we can't learn to love one another, we should at least learn to live with one another.

I have crossed bridges and burned bridges. But the ones I most remember are the ones I built: with my wife, my parents, my children, my friends and all those I love. We speak of creation as if it were solely God's domain. A bridge we build is not created by God but by the heart and mind of man with a spark of divinity.

Insight from the night…

After a lecture, people won't remember the volume of words and rarely even the content. What they retain is the passion and conviction of the speaker. They remember the effect it has upon them, especially the emotion it evokes from them.

Some people emerge from college with the skills to showcase their intelligence. But because they don't exit college any more intelligent than entering, some only acquire the skills to better conceal their stupidity.

Emily Dickinson….

She found eternal truths in small places

and intricacies in the simple and overlooked.

She arranged her words to fit a mood.

We find her sentences obscure

but then so were her moods.

A large enterprise, when good, cannot only pump out great sums of money, it can, when bad, more quickly suck out the cash from the pockets of its unfortunate investors.

Business start-uppers fail not because they run out of gas, but because they run out of cash, before reaching their goal. Cash is the lord of industry. Where it goes, so follows all of its worshippers.

Sometimes we lose an argument because the other side is better at lying than we are at telling the truth.

In football, you don't give out trophies based on statistics because it's not always the team with the best players that wins. It's the team with the players who play their best on game day.

Television is a way of meeting so many wonderful people without having to get to know them.

A carpenter creates by merely rearranging the wood to fit his idea.

The same can be done with words, for a similar purpose. A beautiful structure of sentences, hammered together one word at a time, will neither fade nor age, nor slide into disrepair, but serves forever as home for the mind seeking shelter from a raging storm of obfuscation.

It took millions of years for the life force of nature to create the modern man. It is no wonder that he is so greatly in love with himself. Whatever it was that experimented with so many variations, built him one cell at a time, systemized the assemblage to the point of procreation, and arranged all parts to serve the whole, must still exist within him. He is the sparkle in nature's eye and the pride of its achievement. What troubles him most is that he is the **art** and not the **artist**.

It is a paradox that we are fond of those who practice law and yet hate lawyers. Lawyers have to work in sets of two, each arguing only one side of an issue. Each of them is only half complete, while the two together are essential in the expression of justice.

A question's value is derived from the source as well as the substance. Men ask themselves, *Do I believe in God?* God replies, *Do I believe in man?*

Printers earn their living by making a piece of paper more interesting.

In the creative arena, what's the difference between good and great? The Beatles created great music. Shakespeare, Disney, Plato, and Lincoln were great. Why? Because even their bad stuff was good.

The scientist who claims there is no **why** in the universe might as well be a computer, a gatherer of facts and figures. The real scientist doesn't claim what he seeks to prove, but proves his claim.

The Great Creator…

Some may argue that a creation implies a creator. You can't have a complex and beautiful world without a great creator. But who created the creator? The creator they say was not created and has always existed. Then, by that reasoning, it is just as logical to say the universe was not created but has existed forever. Thus, the argument that proves the great creator also disproves it and we are back to the place where we began.

Let's follow a different route.

My syllogism for an eternal intelligence in the universe…

The premise is that *something cannot come from nothing* or, *only something breeds something.*

Therefore the universe (*something*) or any of its transformations, has either existed forever or was created by something that has existed forever.

Intelligence, as evidenced by our living example, has either existed forever or was created by an intelligence that has existed forever.

In either case, intelligence in some form is eternal. Thus, there exists an intelligence – call it God, the Great Spirit, or Mother Nature - that never goes out of existence.

Q.E.D.

Where manure is scattered, things will grow. Thus, even a sales convention has its merits.

Talent may get you in the game but passion wins it.

Work to win the game if you can play the game.

Work to change games if you can't.

The object of any game is not to be a great player. The object is to win. Great players know this. So too do great cheaters.

Guns....

Never just bring the voice of reason to a gun fight. Reason is easily silenced. By keeping guns in the hands of good guys, the bad guys lose their advantage. If we were all angels, the gun, as a form of protection, would quickly become obsolete. That utopia never was and never will be. Injustice and danger are all around. Pretending otherwise is naive. We don't just live in a world of *should and shouldn't*. We also live in a world of *is and isn't*.

The uncommon BIG words can be used to enrich language, more accurately express an idea, and unfortunately, help mask a poor intellect.

The scrawny twisted evergreen tree, when embellished with bright beautiful ornaments, hides the feeble frame which supports it all.

Independence...

Follow a crowd and always be lost in a crowd.

In negotiating, always represent your **want** with the other guy's **need**.

If that gets switched, you lose.

Loyalty is like a coin, a two-sided coin. On one side, the good side, we have loyalty to family, to friends, and to an employer. This side of loyalty is commendable. But on the other side is a blind loyalty to a dishonest friend or corrupt employer or even a country where Nazi's are in charge. So loyalty can only be a virtue when its other face is flipped down.

NEVER pass a law or take a medication that isn't absolutely necessary. When in doubt, don't do it. An unnecessary law is like a poison in the body. In the cure of one ailment you cause another. The side effects alone can finish you off. If we ever abdicate a freedom to solve a problem, it had better be a BIG problem.

There is no need to worship God or praise God, only to recognize God. He doesn't need your support. And don't place yourself completely in God's hands. He placed the world in your hands. You are at least partly responsible for how it all turns out.

If **Justice** is blind then **Truth** is deaf.

You can't change the truth by shouting at it.

Observation and analysis…

Some truths you find in front of your nose and others you find behind it.

You don't marry someone because you want to live **with** them. There are a lot of attractive people in this world I could live with.

You marry someone because you can't live **without** them. The foundation of marriage is not personality, sex, race or religion.

The foundation of marriage is **love**.

A marriage of love is quite different from a marriage of minds.

The rules of addition are like adding together two drops of water:

$$1 + 1 = 1.$$

The foundation of all our knowledge is not logic but **faith**, and not just the religious kind. We have faith that the world we wake up to each morning is basically the same one we said goodnight to. We have faith the sun will rise tomorrow and the next day and the next. **Certainty**, at least for us in this life time, is an **illusion**.

Be very selective in placing food into your body. And above all else, never use your stomach as a trash can just to feel good. Eat slowly and think about your food as you ingest it. Make exercise a daily routine. Do a walk before dinner, or after dinner, or instead of dinner. You only have one body and you have to live in it all the way to the end.

Doggerel of the Day....
Those who seek a higher peak
Are respected for their guts.
Those who dwell within a shell
Are commonly known as nuts.

I do not gaze into the face of existence and

see only despair. I see a mirror reflecting

something very real. The reality is **me**. The

foundation of all that is real for us is ourselves. You can be sure of

nothing else.

Dreams may be false, but not the dreamer.

For you can have dreamers without dreams, but not dreams without dreamers.

The difference between the pleasures of money and of chocolate is
that, with enough chocolate, you eventually become full.

I don't like to brag but nobody's perfect and I'm a nobody.

Nietzsche says that what is done out of love is beyond good and evil. And without love, we lack motivation for morality, even if we do recognize right from wrong.

To act on our conscience, we must love what is good and despise what is bad. If we get that part wrong, or we just don't care, the light from all the suns in the cosmic heaven will not illuminate our minds to seek one path over another.

I can't imagine being happy at a very old age. I would rather be switched off like a light bulb than be left to spoil on a plate like brown aging mushy fruit. Life is sweet when our bodies are young and our senses keen. But once the fog of excess time sweeps over the mind and obscures the clarity of thought, the world is no longer our green garden of youthful dreams and calculated possibilities. As we fade into old old age, it is not the sun that fails us, but the light that cruelly dims from within.

On abortion...

The question everyone needs answered, I suppose, is: *When is a human being first human?* Is it at conception or at birth? Is it when the little ingrates return after four years of college with a show of appreciation for their parents?

The question really becomes: *When does the human being acquire his soul?* The soul, of course, is what makes us godlike, separates us from God's other creatures (whom we slaughter and cook for dinner), and allows us to swagger all the way to heaven (on a full stomach).

The concept of the soul is actually too metaphysical to comprehend for all but the self-anointed.

Another approach would be to ask: *Is it ever right to terminate a life?* One of ongoing pain and suffering without hope might request a *mercy killing.* A life guilty of a heinous crime might deserve a *judicial killing.*

But terminating a life does not mean terminating a soul. If it truly is a divine substance, only a god can do that.

So is a human first human at conception? And if a zygote, the fertilized egg, is a human, is not birth control a sin against the potential human? How far do we carry an argument based on an uncertain assumption?

Is an acorn an oak tree, or a piece of lumber a chair? An egg has all the DNA of a chicken, but a scrambled egg is not the same thing as a dead chicken.

No scientist can tell us when the soul floats into the body if undetectable in the lab. The truth is, I don't know when a human being is first human and I don't trust those who claim they do.

But we should not take abortion lightly. At some point it <u>is</u> the killing of life. The common sense approach is like deciding if a strange plant will be poisonous to eat: *if you are not sure, it would be wise to avoid it.*

It is strange and interesting how others are touched when we reach deep within ourselves to express what we discern as a truth. It is as if all living things share a common life spirit, and within this spirit dwells a common understanding.

Kindness is a gift. You had a choice. You chose to be kind. It was an option not everyone would pick. How great are the few who can decide such things.

Only give power to people who love other things more. Otherwise, they may not give it back.

If you want to know a lot of successful people, then help the people you already know to prosper. The ones who are now successful probably don't need your friendship.

The Irony of Heaven…

Most religions teach us that good deeds are rewarded, if not on earth, then ultimately in heaven. Evil may triumph in this life but not in the next. Heaven is our compensation for living a moral life. But if we do a good deed in expectation of payment, is it really a moral act? Is it not done in self-interest? Socrates, Plato, and Jesus all argued that to know the good is to do the good, if we could only clearly see the entire picture. Platonic thought was more secular than Christian theology, but fundamentally similar in motivation. They all believed it was nonsense to expect people to act in any way contrary to their self-interest. Selfishness was a given and morality had to be defined within that framework. But is that morality or just enlightened self-interest? At least Jesus recognized that objectively what is good for me may not be good for others and, furthermore, I cannot always be assured of my reward in this life.

But when I selfishly do the right thing, or at least what I believe to be the right thing, is it really a moral act? Am I not just doing what is best for me? To be defined as a moral act, I must recognize it as such and act, not from self-interest, but from a duty to do what is right. The irony is that to act morally we must do what is right because, and only because, it is the right thing to do. If getting to heaven is our motivation, then it ceases to be a moral act, although the act is no less diminished in virtue. These ideas were developed over 200 years ago by Immanuel Kant, who was both kind and cruel. He enlightened us as to morality but at the same time exposed our hypocrisy. In other words, don't get a sore arm patting yourself on the back until you realize your true motives.

The world will never be safe for dictators as long as there is one free soul left in it.

Half of living is a cool head, a steady hand, and a perceptive eye. Brains and talent, though important, are by themselves weak in comparison, and cower in the shade of the brave.

On Leadership ….

Hire the right people.

Communicate the vision.

And then get the hell out of their way.

The problem of the self-absorbed person is that he sees the world as a mirror rather than a window.

Why do long legged people get so much respect? Is the view from above so much more enlightened?

I'm a tall person with short legs, who sits tall but stands short. And if I build a box to stand on to raise myself above the crowd, they still won't be interested in me. They'll just want my box.

For every problem there is a guy who will bring it to your attention but has no solution. This way, no matter what happens, he can say, " I told you so. " Then there is the guy who offers one, but it's the wrong solution. Don't ever put that guy in charge without close supervision. The guy who has the ability to think through all the options and find the best solution is the one to follow. How do you recognize him? Everyone will explain why their solution will work, but only he can explain why everyone else's solution won't work.

The hole shapes the donut as much as the donut shapes the hole. And so it goes, without nothing (the hole) we cannot have anything (the donut). And the answer to the age-old question *Why is there something rather than nothing?* is that there are both. The universe is replete with opposites: hot-cold, straight-curves, electrons-positrons, good-evil, life-death, something-nothing. Opposites complement and shape one another. Opposites create force, which is the energy of the universe. To truly define something is to know its opposite. The opposite of every beginning is its end and, for this bit of nonsense, this is it.

Metamorphosis…

Women tend to pass through distinct and very different phases in life. First there is the little girl: curious, mischievous, adventurous. She then blossoms into a beautiful, sexy, love-obsessed emotional animal that drives the young lads to matrimony.

Next is the transformation into motherhood where she nurtures, protects, teaches, disciplines, and selflessly guides her offspring through childhood.

At the last stage, she becomes the old lady, perhaps a grandmother, who finds a new freedom from all the earlier stages.

Men, on the other hand, start out as mischievous, competitive, playful boys and remain so for the rest of their lives. Thank goodness they have women to help guide them into old age.

No matter how smart people are, there's a streak of dumb ass that runs through us all (if you pardon the Texas vernacular).

Three reasons to publish posthumously:
1) if readers don't like it, you won't subject yourself
to ridicule, which is hard to bear;
2) if they *do* like it, their focus will be on you as
much as your work which to me would be uncomfortable; and,
3) you can make changes all the way to the end.

Some people say, "The poor will always be with us," and that is bad.

But I say, "The **threat** of being poor should always be with us," and that's not all bad.

One by-product of being old is there is little difference in feeling victory or in feeling defeat. You just want to feel something.

We are living proof that there is intelligence in the universe. We know intelligence cannot emerge from nothing, just as we know that love, justice, beauty, and life itself cannot evolve from nothing. Nothing is bred from nothing.

We are what we are in a place that is real only because there was a past that created it.

Small minds want to be consistent while great minds seek to be in balance. Historians one hundred years from now will say that John Kennedy stood up to communism with brilliant rhetoric, defining our goals to be free and independent people. At the same time he pushed for greater government involvement in health care, poverty, and education. He was a walking contradiction. They will judge his grandest achievement to be setting us in motion to land men on the moon by the summer of 1969, a remarkable accomplishment under the leadership of the federal government. He was also a model husband and family man who just happened to carry on affairs with a number of women. He was indeed a walking contradiction as he struggled to put his life into balance.

The noble judge will pledge his allegiance to the human race, not a particular race of humans.

The ultimate goal of the capitalist is to corner the market. And the irony is that, if he is allowed to monopolize, he will destroy the very system that enriches him.

The ultimate social goal of capitalism is to efficiently provide services and products to customers. Making managers and workers happy is merely a means to an end. If workers can control a company through coercive union organization, the tail wags the dog and the dog wobbles.

The war wages within.

Isn't that what's really going on here:

The self-centeredness of our

nature battling the objectivity of our mind.

The part of us who wins will define us, not to the outside world,
but to the one within.

Poor Shakespeare...

He could write plays about the events of the world, but he could not take part in the governing of it. The queen had locked him out and jealously guarded the door. Even his true identity, Edward DeVere, 17th Earl of Oxford, was hidden from the public eye as if it were a communicable disease. He was allowed only to act out a dramatization of the noble life. The real parts were left to others.

We remember the world a better place when we were young not because it was really better but because we were young. Our young world was exciting, mysterious and new because we were.

Snow skiing requires new equipment and young legs. It is a young person's sport and an older person's hobby.

Do not worry too much about the animosity of others. Most people just don't care enough about you to be your enemy. They may be envious of you or just plain don't like you. But mostly they are apathetic to you. They pursue self-interest and you become the enemy only when and while you are in their way. Once you step aside, they once again just don't care.

We are born individuals. No one gives birth to a committee in a natural way. Individualism is the foundation of morality and spirituality. We own nothing unless we own our own lives. Collectivism is a form of slavery that destroys the soul. For when we all own everything and we are all responsible for everything collectively, then no one is responsible for anything. The **we** can only be good if it retains the *I*. You either have a nation of individuals, each working and creating a better life for themselves, or you have an anthill of ants, non-thinking servants to the hill.

Intelligence is greatly overrated as a virtue. If I have to live or work around someone every day, I'll take the **honest** person over the **brainy** one. The smart one who can't be trusted will eventually get to you, no matter how cautious you are. In the end, what matters most is not that you are an intelligent person. What matters is that you are a good person.

If you put ten economists in the same room and asked each to predict the financial future, they almost certainly will have ten different opinions.

The moral is: When an economist predicts the future, at least nine out of ten times he's wrong.

Change is not always good, though it is often packaged and sold as that. One man's version of progress is another's definition of decline. Some people would not be satisfied with heaven until they reformed it to look more like hell.

Those businesses that don't train are held hostage by their employees. Those that don't market are held hostage by their customers.

If you want a cute and silly conversation, you talk with a child.
If you want a shallow and polite one, you converse with a stranger.
If you want a descriptive factual one, you chat with a friend.
If you want a truthful, in-depth conversation, you consult with **yourself**.

Be cautious in supporting someone who stands with you on the issues but is of poor character.
His character will become the issue.

The real expert is the one who has made many mistakes, not the one who deals with the theoretical. It's OK to jump into the fray and get your nose bloodied. You don't have to win all your fights, but you do need to show up. The school of hard knocks teaches knowledge fortified with experience.

The Internet is like the backyard fence 100 years ago. There's a lot of bull going over the boards, and you can't depend on any of it being true.

A good artist gives to the world what he considers worthy, regardless of the world's needs. He sometimes starves.

A good businessperson gives to the world what the world wants, and is rewarded accordingly.

Government should be very careful when paying people for not working, or else it may end up with an economy that's not working.

What annoys me is not that you are wrong, but that you are so damn sure of being right.

The wrong-headed people are not always wrong.
And the right-headed aren't always right, of course.
So the levelheaded ones must ponder the issue,
And judge each by its shape and not its source.

Think.
Feel.
Be free.
Be real.
Be.

Behind every enterprise large or small is a person who has trouble sleeping at night.

Happiness involves realistic collaboration of the sexes.

My advice to men is to find a woman to live with. You can't be happy and live without them when most men are born with an addiction to them. And treat your woman better than she deserves. She will instinctively realize she is being treated well in spite of shortcomings and will be grateful and stick around knowing it would be difficult to find another crazy guy like you.

My advice to women is, if you are born beautiful, it's sort of like being born rich. That won't guarantee happiness. It helps, but beauty must be supplemented with a good heart or it becomes a tool in the wrong hands. And if you are a woman born homely, there are two things that might help overcome this defect. The first is to stay thin. You may not be able to control genetics, but you can control your figure. The second is to be nice. A thin shapely woman with a good heart is very attractive to most men.

Little we know of love but that it befalls us.
Love is never created. It just occurs.

Hearing words well said is like buckets of warm water poured over your naked frozen body in the middle of frigid winter. You shiver in exultation.

Fundamentally, I'm as ignorant as the day I was born. The classic questions: *Who am I? What am I doing here? Where am I going?* echo back to me as if the universe were an empty room. But we need not completely understand life to live it. Thought should precede action, not replace it.

Using science to try to find God is like a goldfish exploring every corner of its rather large fish tank to find the ocean.

The Gift of Freedom…

Long ago in Baghdad there lived a wealthy man named Boton who was blessed with many friends and a loving family. He paid tribute to God in prayer each morning in appreciation of his fortunate life. One day a friend announced that in the market was a golden lamp. And within this lamp was a genie with great powers. For years Boton had resisted the desire to acquire more possessions but was intrigued with this story of new treasure.

After a long day and exhausting search he came upon the merchant who had such a lamp. And to his surprise was offered the prize for a modest sum. The merchant seemed relieved of a great burden and as he walked away, cautioned Boton of the devious power that lay within. But with excitement Boton stroked the lamp, and as foretold, the genie appeared. Now, as master of the lamp, Boton was granted three wishes. But what would he wish for? This successful gentleman of Baghdad always seemed so contented with life. He pondered his choices. *I desire neither health nor wealth nor wisdom nor friends, for all these I have in abundance. I must seek out something greater. Something that will change the world.* He selected his words carefully.

I wish for God to appear before the peoples of the world so that we can live the rest of our lives without doubt as to His existence.

My second wish is for God to show us each day the path of righteousness. And finally, *I wish for God to remove all evil from this world so that all will be good.*

Now a genie's great power, as with all gifts, comes as a blessing only from God. And some say prayers are answered and wishes fulfilled by a mysterious divine intervention. This was such a time. Boton's three wishes were instantly granted. And just as wind can suddenly change its course, so too did the lives of every person on earth.

Boton, pleased with his good work, placed the lamp in his pocket and returned home. He expected a warm greeting from his fellow townspeople as an architect of goodness and peace. But to his surprise, his friends were shocked and distressed when they learned of his deed. They shunned him and forced him to leave.

How can this be good? he asked. But it must be. For this is now a world perfect in its goodness.

Wandering the countryside, he reflected on how his world was completely transformed. With the first wish, God's existence was certain, removing all spiritual mystery. With the second, people lost control of their lives and became distraught.

With the third wish, no one could do a bad deed to another. The thrill, fun and adventure of life disappeared. The world became predictable and boring. The people lost interest.

Finally Boton pulled the lamp from his pocket and demanded in desperation three more wishes from the genie. The magical spirit agreed but with one condition: Boton must grant the genie a request in return. The once happy family man of Baghdad could not refuse.

Boton's initial wish was to undo the first three. And just as a dream dissipates in the morning air, the perfect world vanished from the memories of everyone. His second was that the genie never grant such wishes to anyone. His third wish was to be once again accepted by his townspeople so that he could live out his life in peace and happiness. After all were promptly accorded, the genie softly uttered his own request. *Take my golden lamp in your boat to the middle of the sea where the depth is great and toss it into the dark waters where it can never be retrieved.*

But why, asked Boton, *would you desire to be hidden forever from mankind?* The genie glared into Boton's sad eyes. *Because you live your lives searching and wishing for the wrong things. And I can only do harm by giving you what you foolishly believe you want.*

Boton did what was asked and returned to his home where he lived in peace for the rest of his days. Satisfied that life was mysterious, unpredictable and free, he vowed for evermore not to alter the ways of the world, but to improve himself instead.

Epilogue:

The price of freedom, it is said, is eternal vigilance. But the other price we pay for being free is human vulnerability. If we are to be granted freedom, we must be placed at the whims of chance. Terrible things are allowed to happen to good people. We don't always get what we want or even deserve. Instead we get **freedom**.

It can be no other way.

No one is expected to know everything about everything or how to act and react in all circumstances. Intelligence and knowledge are developed over time through experience. Even though thinking and learning can be hard work, never stop asking serious questions. *It is the satisfaction of ignorance that makes it a fault.*

In growing older, as the mystery of life diminishes, the magic remains. I understand so much more of the details. It's the overall view that remains a miracle.

To be human is to be capable of loving individuals. Humanitarians seem to love humanity in general. If you must choose to be one or the other, human or humanitarian, I would pick human. Individuals are real. The other is merely a concept.

Thoughts come and go.
It's the after-thought that sticks.

There are two political camps: the socialists and the individualists. The first believe, if we all share and work together, we can accomplish so much more than if we go it alone. The second is convinced that it is not in our nature to behave like ants or bees. Our natural disposition is to be free, and we must limit government power in order to retain some element of that freedom. The socialists strive for collective responsibility and benefits. The individualists are worldly enough to realize that when everyone is responsible for something then no one is accountable. There must be single source accountability and responsibility. Social morality is as much a myth as mob morality.

Individualists will argue that a just society is created by ethical individuals, not the other way around. The socialist believes everyone will work to create a great society. The individualist understands that great communities are built by free people working in their own self-interest, making a better world while bettering themselves.

The individualist fears government domination. The socialist fears domination by successful individuals.

Both political camps are needed to strike a balance between social controls and individual freedom.

Excessive freedom without limits or controls would be as dangerous as a repressive government without freedom. Good societies as well as good individuals are only good when they are in balance. Both political camps are necessary to gain this balance, but it is essential that neither camp dominates. Competition indeed brings out the best in us, but leaves us with winners and losers. Ironically, the winners often try to fix the game to lessen competition. The less successful ones, through sheer numbers, must never allow that to happen.

So the struggle continues. Whether with government, religion, gender, or social networks, the organization will try to dominate the individual in the name of some social good. Every generation must push back and achieve their own balance for their own time for their own sake.

The only equality in this world is death. When we die, rich or poor, beautiful or ugly, famous or infamous, we are equally dead. On the other hand, life loves inequality and nature's diversity gives it more options to survive. Group inequality improves group quality. High achievers bring progress to the masses. All life is valuable but not equally so. Those who pursue and achieve excellence are at a higher level than others. Income inequality is the necessary result of outcome inequality. Those who seek equality are not reaching for justice, but suffer from envy. It's an excuse to take rather than to make. It's a lazy life for the uninspired. Thus, society would be wise to keep the playing field equal, not the players.

Is the physical world real and the spiritual one an illusion? Or is it the other way around? Are not rocks and buildings and our own bodies composed of tiny subatomic particles flying around each other? Is not energy itself a part of the physical world? Then we cannot measure reality by what is seen. What we see is mere manifestation of another less visible reality. Good, evil, truth, mendacity... only appear in our actions. They are not physical reality, but they do exist, and are as real as any rock. Not everything real casts a shadow.

Absorption vs. Digestion...

Remembering what you read is called "absorption". Understanding this information and applying it in your own way with your own thoughts is called "digestion". Only through digestion do we furnish nutrients to all parts of the body and grow to be a source of energy rather than its reflection.

As a young man, I was a liberal and believed in taxing the hell out of the other guy for the glory of government. And as I became more prosperous, I realized I had become the other guy. This changed my entire perspective.

"Rules are made for people who can't think."

That's an old saying I learned in the Navy. It's just as true, of course, that you can't run a Navy without rules. One of the earliest and most famous list of rules was the Ten Commandments. My personal theory is that Moses went up on that mountain and carved those Ten Commandments with his own hands. As a great leader in tough times, he devised a method to hold his people together using a simple list of ethical guidelines. And if it were to be just simply "Moses' List", it would not have been received with the same authority as if it had come from God's hand. A political fight would have ensued.

I'm sure all of this occurred to him during a prayer with God. The plan to submit the stone tablet as a creation directly from God was, to Moses, God's idea and thus God's will.

During my tenure on earth, I've never seen God change water into wine or inscribe rules onto rock. But I have witnessed almost incredibly virtuous acts from individuals inspired by a belief in God. John Kennedy said it best: "On earth, God's work must truly be our own." I believe *something* speaks *to* us by speaking *through* us, and that all humans have a sense of spiritual goodness that is either suppressed or expressed as we so choose.

As rational beings, we must acknowledge the uncertainty of everything around us while retreating to the certainty of what is within each of us. Even if lost at sea, we must keep everyone paddling together in the same direction. That's why the Navy has all those rules.

Freedom, like wealth, is best appreciated when earned.

Losing wealth is like losing an egg.

Losing freedom is losing the hen that lays the egg.

Before wealth or fame seek wisdom. Why?

Because human beings without wisdom might as well be livestock.

Paraphrasing Socrates…

If we see our purpose in life as creating happiness rather than taking it from others, then.....

it is better to suffer a wrong that shames another than to commit a wrong that shames ourselves.

Try not to bring into the world what you want less of.

When you examine infinity, all options however slight are not just possible. All options are certain. Given an eternity, all things that **can** happen **will** happen and will happen an infinite number of times.

The finish of the world is but signal to begin, for a universe that made life once, can surely make it once again.

Following college, Stephen Morris served in the Navy a short time
as a Nuclear Weapons Officer.

He then went on to found several successful businesses including a
national franchise of printing and

graphics centers. He currently resides with his wife in Florida.

Please send your comments to:

ThoughtResponse@gmail.com

www.ingramcontent.com/pod-product-compliance
Lightning Source LLC
Chambersburg PA
CBHW072014150726
47999CB00002B/656